FASTEN YOUR FAITH

A 30-DAY GUIDE TO SECURING A VICTORIOUS LIFE IN CHRIST

BREANA J. SMITH

TO:

_____

FROM:

_____

DATE:

_____

Contents

Prologue

Everyone is taught to fasten their seatbelts whenever they get behind the wheel. Despite the fact that buckling up is drilled into our heads, the National Highway Traffic Safety Administration's latest study reports nearly 27.5 million people neglect to do so. That's a lot of people driving around unprotected. Imagine the stats if the administration collected their data worldwide. The fact is, an accident could happen anywhere at any time and the consequences of failing to fasten one's seatbelt could be dire.

We are all guilty of not wearing our seatbelts from time to time, even though the strap is in plain sight. I am convinced we do the same thing with our faith. Faith is something that cannot be seen, and therefore, it is hard to gauge if we have properly secured ourselves in God. Just like you need to put on your seatbelt every time you get into a vehicle, you cannot afford to live off of yesterday's faith.

When I did not fasten my faith belt, I constantly walked around in defeat. I operated primarily out of fear, I entertained negative thinking and I was unhappy with my life, even though I called myself a believer.

Since I have started slowing down to fasten my faith belt every day, my life has drastically changed. I no longer panic when difficult situations arise, I don't question God's love for me and God's blessings continue to hit me from left and right.

I challenge you to take this 30-day ride of purposefully fastening your faith belt. Let God have his way in your life so you can live the life you were destined to live—a life of unending favor, blessing and victory.

God is Real

But without faith it is impossible to please Him, for
he that comes to God must believe that He is, and that
He is a rewarder of them that diligently seek him.
-Hebrews 11:6, NKJV

I remember hearing a preacher say that a lot of us are closer to atheism, as opposed to Christianity, than we think. At this point in his message, he was talking to Christ-followers to emphasize the lack of trust we may have in regard to God's ability to come through for us in various circumstances. Unfortunately, I think that preacher was right.

Christians should never be compared to atheists in terms of belief. Atheists do not believe God's word at all. They refuse to pray because they believe God is not real. A lot of atheists make statements like, "If God was real why would he allow bad things to happen to me or to others?"

As believers, we should know without a shadow of a doubt that God is real and that he loves us. He is our Heavenly Father and he came to this earth to die for us and to save us from the bondage of sin and ultimately from sin altogether. God is more than a higher power in the sky.

If Jesus went through the trouble to die for us, why would he abandon us or allow us to roam aimlessly upon this earth without a purpose? The Bible says, "For the eyes of the Lord run to and fro throughout the whole earth, to show Himself strong on behalf of those whose heart is loyal to Him" (2 Chron:16:9). His word proclaims that he is ready to bless those that love him. All he wants us to do is believe he is who he says he is.

Fasten Your Faith

- Examine yourself to release any false ideologies you might have about God.
- Pledge your allegiance to God today.
- Recall how God "shows himself strong" in your life.

God Empowers You

I can do all things through Christ who strengthens me.
-Philippians 4:13, NKJV

While I attended Bowling Green State University, my college town pastor used the analogy of two dogs in a fight to describe the battle that goes on inside of everyone. One dog is the spirit man and the other dog represents the flesh. He said, "Whichever one you feed the most will always win. We need to feed our spirit by abiding in Christ, while starving our flesh by dying to ourselves. When we die to self, we give the spirit man permission to abide and be at the forefront in our lives."

Abiding in Christ is achieved by communing with him through reading and meditating on his word, applying his word, praying without ceasing and fasting on a daily basis. When life gets busy, these things tend to go on the backburner, and that is when the flesh regains the upper hand. As we abide in Christ one day at a time, victory over our sinful nature is a natural result. God's way of thinking takes precedence as our fleshly wants and our desires dissolve.

At the end of our lives, we will have the confidence to say we lived our lives pleasing God. God in turn will say, "Well done, thy good and faithful servant." That is what offering ourselves up as a living sacrifice looks like.

FASTEN YOUR FAITH

- Ask yourself whether the flesh or spirit is in control today. Make the necessary changes if you are unhappy with your initial answer.
- Fast from something you hold dear. (i.e., food, television, social media).
- Pray that God will make his desires your desires.

God has a Plan for You

For I know the thoughts that I think toward
you, says the Lord, thoughts of peace and not
of evil, to give you a future and a hope.
-Jeremiah 29:11, NKJV

I thought I would automatically get a job in my field upon graduating college. Like a lot of people in my shoes, I was wrong. The months seemed to fly by, and still no job. I was heartbroken. I spent hours applying for jobs and did not even receive a rejection response. I heard nothing. I was supposed to be in the prime of my life, yet I was living in my parent's house with no job. I thought it was so unfair.

Little did I know, my mother ended up falling into a deep depression around the same time. She lost her job and at one point, she was even hospitalized for a few days. I cooked and kept the house in order for my father and brother when she couldn't. But most of all, I was able to stand beside my mother every day, pray with her every day and speak life over her every day. Now, my mother is better than ever. She has a new job that she enjoys, is in the process of getting her master's degree and started her own Bible study to help other women pursue God.

The Lord knew my family needed my physical presence at that point in their lives. I thought not getting a job in my field was a disaster, but God had good intentions for me. Instead of giving me a high-profile career, he gave me something better. He gave me my mother.

FASTEN YOUR FAITH

- Confess whatever disappointments you have to the Lord.
- Look for the Lord's providence in your life.
- Pray and ask the Lord to help you submit to him.

God Speaks to You

Your ears shall hear a word behind you, saying,
"This is the way, walk in it," Whenever you turn to
the right hand or whenever you turn to the left.
-Isaiah 30:21, NKJV

We are bombarded with making choices every day. A lot of choices are so menial that they come as second nature to us. We choose what to wear, what to eat, what to watch, what to read, etc. For the most part, these choices do not have huge ramifications if we decide to do them or not. On the other hand, there are some cases where we come to a fork in the road and we would rather avoid making a decision altogether. These decisions could be positive yet hard, like choosing the right school to attend, career to pursue, or spouse to marry.

No matter how overwhelming our choices may be, I am thankful we always have the option to choose the correct path. God said, "It doesn't matter what point you are in your life; I'm always going to point you in the way you should go. I'm constantly talking to my sheep but you have to learn to listen to my voice. It's a still small voice, a whisper to your soul. I do not want to yell and force you to go in the way I'm leading you. I want you to freely follow me into the paths of righteousness, even when it doesn't make sense to you. This is the way, walk ye in it." (Isa 30:21, Josh 10:27, 1 Kings 19: 11-13, Ps 32:9, Jos 24:14-15).

FASTEN YOUR FAITH

- Spend a few minutes in silence to hear God's voice today.
- Ask the Lord to help you take responsibility for the choices you make.
- Thank the Lord for giving you the ability to choose (free will).

God Provides for You

But seek first the kingdom of God and his righteousness,
and all these things shall be added to you.
-Matthew 6:33, NKJV

After the honeymoon ended, reality set in for my husband and me. Together, we had so much student loan debt that I started to panic about our future. So many things ran through my mind. Will we ever be able to own a home? Will we be able to save for retirement? Is it wise to have kids with this much debt? If we did, how would we take care of them? Would they be able to go to college? To make a long story short, I came up with every negative scenario I could think of.

One day, we went to visit my uncle, who is a pastor, and of course, we shared our concerns with him. All he said was, "The Lord will provide." He said it with experiential assurance. He shared story after story with us about how the Lord took care of all his needs.

Again he said, "The Lord will provide." If the Lord said it, he will do it. We do not have to worry about tomorrow because he is our security, not money. As a matter of fact, God said we cannot serve both God and money because we will cling to one and hate the other.

Now, every time I face a new situation, especially a financial one, and thoughts begin to bombard my mind, I remember my uncle's statement of how the Lord will provide. He came through for my uncle, and he will do the same for me and you.

FASTEN YOUR FAITH

- Ask God to show you your place in his Kingdom.
- Pray to God about truly seeking his righteousness.
- List how God provided for you this week.

6

Your Life is Valuable

And He said to them, "Take heed, and beware
of covetousness, one's life does not consist in the
abundance of the things he possesses."
-Luke 12:15, NKJV

Out of all the funeral services I've attended, I've never heard people describe the possessions their loved one owned. What is mentioned is the person's character, who they loved and what they loved to do. This principle is very apparent at the end of our lives, but a lot of people miss this concept during their life.

Nowadays, a host of people are trying to keep up with the Jones's. Well, for a millennial like me, we'd prefer to keep up with our "friends" on Facebook and who we follow on Instagram. The dilemma is the fact that people can paint whatever picture they want on social media. If you spend too much time scrolling through your feed, you might leave your friend's page wanting their lives and despising your own.

When I do not guard my mind and check my motives, I notice that I start falling back into the trap of subliminally competing against others through these various outlets. Just because you cannot go on a vacation or eat at a fancy restaurant every night does not mean you are missing out or your life is less important.

It boils down to what being successful looks like. In the world's eyes, success is about attaining—getting the perfect job, the perfect house, and completing your bucket list. In Jesus's eyes, it is about becoming. He wants us to become more like him in our walk, in our talk and in how we treat others. Strive to live your life according to Jesus's standard and not according to how the world thinks you should live.

FASTEN YOUR FAITH

- Write down your vision of success. Now ask the Lord if your image of success matches his.
- Ask the Lord to help you recognize when you are coveting.
- Ask the Lord to help you appreciate all you have.

Your Season is Coming

*And let us not grow weary while doing good, for in
due season we shall reap if we do not lose heart.*
-Galatians 6:9, NKJV

Life can seem so unfair at times. It is tough when you are trying to live right but things still don't seem to pan out for you. You may feel overlooked because you didn't get the job you interviewed for, you dreamed of being married by a certain date, or you discovered your close friend betrayed you. It feels like God is upset with you for some reason and he is blessing everyone but you.

Naomi felt the same way. She traveled to a distant land with her family in hopes of a better life and ended up empty-handed. Her husband and her two sons died. The only thing she had left was her daughters-in-law, Orpah and Ruth, and out of them, only Ruth decided to stay with her. Although she thought God was punishing her for some reason, she kept her faith and traveled back to the land of Bethlehem (the land of God) with Ruth.

God honored Naomi's faithfulness to him through Ruth. Ruth loved Naomi like her own mother. She worked every day in the field, gathering leftover crops from the harvesters and sharing everything she got with Naomi. Naomi did not have to lift a finger. Ruth did all the hard work. Ruth obeyed Naomi when she told Ruth to ask Boaz to step in as their kinsman redeemer, which is a relative volunteering to marry to become the provider when a close family member dies.

Naomi was still in the picture and took care of Ruth's baby as her very own. All the heartache and loss Naomi endured was replaced by overwhelming joy. For Naomi, the harvest of blessing was Ruth, and she was with her the entire time.

God always sends a blessing through people, and you never know who or when that will be. Your only job is to continue doing what you know is the right thing to do. Continue reading your Bible, praying, and treating others as you would like to be treated. Just like Naomi, you will reap a harvest of blessing at just the right time.

FASTEN YOUR FAITH

- Pray for a good work ethic.
- Pray to see the "Harvest of Blessings" in your life.
- Seek out a person to bless today.

Trials Breed Growth

Consider it all joy, my brethren, when you encounter various trials, knowing that the testing of your faith produces endurance.
-James 1:2-3, NAS

To me, having joy and going through trials seems like an oxymoron. When I think of joy, I think back to when I held my children for the first time, when I got married, got my first car, etc. Time stood still on these occasions in my life, and I put a bookmark of the date in my mind. Trials, on the other hand, are painful. Many people describe the time of trials and testing as the storms of life. Storms destroy. Storms devastate. Storms are dangerous and have people literally picking up the pieces to their lives. So, why does James say, "consider it pure joy," when he wrote this letter? I could understand if he had said, "hold on, my brothers and sisters," but he didn't. He intentionally said the former. How does he expect anyone to do this realistically?

James was simply reiterating what Jesus already stated. In John 16: 33, Jesus said, "In the world, you will have tribulation, but be of good cheer, I have overcome the world." Notice that Jesus said *you will* have tribulation, not *if*. When hard times come your way, understand that you are not the only person in your predicament.

Just as we are to assume tribulations will come, we are to understand that Jesus already won the fight you are up against. Jesus beat sin and death for you and me. We have life in him, and he is coming back to gather his saints to reign with him in a new heaven and a new earth. With this great news, how can anything get you down? If you have already won, there is no point to walk around like you've lost. You might as well enjoy the ride.

FASTEN YOUR FAITH

- Ask the Lord to help you see yourself as a winner.
- Ask the Lord to restore your joy today.
- Ask the Lord to strengthen your faith in him.

God Protects You

The Lord will keep you from all evil; he will keep your life.
-Psalms 121:7, ESV

I'm convinced the Lord blocks certain things from our lives that we are not even aware of. But every now and then, the Lord gives me a glimpse of his ever-flowing protection when I look back at various situations in my life. I say to myself, "Wow! This could've happened or that could've happened, but God!"

Here is a perfect example. It rained unusually hard one day in Cleveland. Although I am used to a lot of rain in Ohio, this time was a little odd to me. I felt like a resident of Florida during hurricane season. Cats and dogs showered down for about half an hour and within minutes, the sky was bright and sunny again.

Fast forward, my parents came over later that day and did not leave until midnight. As they were leaving, we heard a loud explosion and one of our neighbor's garages caught fire. The fire was massive and it was so close that

I could feel the heat and see the embers falling into our yard. We were only two houses over.

Firefighters arrived in a reasonable amount of time to quench the fire but my mind instantly replayed how hard it rained earlier that day. Damp leaves and grass prevented the fire from spreading at a rapid rate. A big boom is what my husband and I would've awakened to if my parents hadn't visited that day, or worse, we could have slept through everything. But God! He knew what was coming ahead of time and protected me, my family and even our belongings.

FASTEN YOUR FAITH

- Recall a time when you knew God was protecting you.
- Thank God for protecting you from things you are not aware of.
- Ask God to awaken your senses in the spiritual realm.

Favoritism is Far From God

But the Lord said to Samuel, "Do not look at his appearance
or at his physical stature, because I have refused him. For
the Lord does not see as man sees; for man looks at the
outward appearance, but the Lord looks at the heart."
-1 Samuel 16:7, NKJV

Our society praises credentials, possessions and social economic statuses so much so that we tend to show partiality without being privy to it. If that is hard to believe, imagine having a choice to spend your day in the shadows of a celebrity or of a homeless person. Wouldn't you opt (or at least be tempted) to cherry-pick the more distinguished person?

Partiality is hard to escape, but we can take notes from the lesson Samuel, the prophet, learned when he showed favoritism. God instructed Samuel to visit the house of Jesse to anoint one of his sons as the new king. Upon arrival, Samuel scanned the room, took one glance at Eliab and assumed he was the chosen one because of his persona. The Lord quickly intervened by telling Samuel he wasn't conducting his search in a godly manner. He was merely looking on the outside and not within.

Samuel was scratching his head by the time he got to David. David did not meet any of the criteria for being a king. He was a shepherd boy and the youngest out of all of Jessie's sons. But God chose David because he was a man after his own heart. Eliab was a soldier. He could have confidently sat on the throne, but he lacked the character and dedication God was looking for.

God is reminding us that anyone (including ourselves) can be used to carry out his kingdom work. He does not wait for us to reach a certain point in our lives to be used by him. Aren't you glad God is not like man?

FASTEN YOUR FAITH

- Confess if you are guilty of showing partiality (favoritism) toward people.
- Ask the Lord to qualify you for a divine assignment.
- Ask the Lord to help you become (or remain) a man or woman after his own heart.

Questions for Reflection

1. What is your favorite meditation so far and why?

2. Have you applied any of these meditations (1-10) to your week? Was there any difference in how you approached your day/week as a result?

3. Has the Lord changed your outlook on what it means to be successful? Explain.

4. Were you a blessing to someone this week? How?

5. How did the Lord protect/provide for you this week?

<u>Reflection Notes</u>

God Always Says Yes

For all the promises of God in Him are Yes, and
in Him Amen, to the glory of God through us.
-2 Corinthians 1:20, NKJV

Some people believe the Lord is mad at them or is ignoring them when they do not seem to get their prayers answered. All they hear is silence. Know that whenever we come to the Lord asking for anything according to his will, his answer is always yes.

Although God's answer is always yes, we have to trust in how he will carry out our yes. We forget that it is according to HIS will and not our own. That can mean the yes does not manifest in the earthly realm until 7 years after your initial prayer. That can mean the yes to your grandmother being healed from cancer is when she goes to the other side of glory, meaning she needs to die in order to not experience pain and to no longer cry tears of sadness. That can mean the yes you know God said to you about having children could be that he wants you to adopt or become a foster parent to a child who is displaced.

Only the Lord can see the entire picture, when all we can see is the negatives in the darkroom of our lives. When the photos of our lives develop, we will understand why the Lord answered our prayers in the manner that he did. He knows what is best for us. It is okay to let your guard down and allow him to be in control. Jesus said, whoever wants to save their life (with their agendas, plans and aspirations) will lose it, but whoever loses their life will find it (Matt 16:25).

F A S T E N Y O U R F A I T H

- Use the model prayer as an outline for your prayer(s). The model prayer can be found in Luke 11:1-4.
- Read James 4:1-3 to recognize if you asked amiss.
- Ask the Lord to help you cope with how he carries out his yes if your prayer(s) are according to his will.

God's Love Shines Brightly

By this all will know that you are My disciples,
if you have love for one another.
-John 13:35, NKJV

On Easter 2017, a man named Steve Stephens came to a mental breaking point in his life, and in execution style, he murdered an innocent elderly man walking past him. To make matters worse, he recorded the events live on his Facebook account. As a result, Stephens was a wanted man and everyone had something bad to say about him; especially reporters.

Correspondents covered the story day and night until the police laid hands on him. When the media interviewed the victim's family, the heartbroken family forgave the killer for what he had done. You could hear a pin drop on national television. Reporters on set and in the field were flabbergasted. They managed to ask how and why the family was able to forgive Stephens for what he had done. The family attributed Jesus as their ability to forgive the man.

The family retaliated with love towards the man, when they could've and should've responded with disgust and anger. The love of Christ lit up a dark situation and covered a multitude of sins, all because a family practiced what they preached.

FASTEN YOUR FAITH

- Show love to someone who does not deserve it.
- Strive to practice what you preach.
- Steer away from an "eye for an eye" or a get-even mentality.

God Does The "Extra" in the Ordinary

But as it is written: "Eye has not seen, nor ear heard,
Nor have entered into the heart of man The things
which God has prepared for those who love him."
-1 Corinthians 2:9-11, NKJV

The Lord is amazing. He promises to take care of our needs but he likes to throw surprise blessings to his children every now and then. I'm the perfect example.

I was performing my typical work duties, which consisted of me filing and scanning, scanning and filing, and more filing and scanning (you get the picture). My co-worker found me and explained that a visitor was looking for me. I walked to the reception area and a man from a local marketing company called me by name and invited me to participate in a commercial they were shooting for the very next day. I said yes and I was obliged to participate.

I thought I would be an extra but to my surprise, the entire commercial revolved around me and they even cut me a check! The commercial aired on all the local television stations and people came up to me asking how I landed that gig. Although I did not become a famous movie star, I had a small platform to share how awesome God is. He blessed me by transforming my ordinary routine into an extraordinary day.

FASTEN YOUR FAITH

- Recall a time when God wowed you. Write down what happened.
- Encourage yourself to stay motivated during the ordinary times in your life.
- Use your platform to share a testimony.

God Never Changes

Jesus Christ is the same yesterday, today, and forever.
-Hebrews 13:8, NKJV

It is comforting to know Jesus never changes, but it is also mind boggling. All we can count on is change. The universe we live in constantly expands and moves. But with the Lord, a day is like a thousand years and a thousand years is like a day. (2 Peter 3:8). He does not miss deadlines or get pressed for time. He always remains the same.

The same God who used Moses to part the Red sea is the same God who is alive and living in your heart. The same God who helped David kill Goliath is the same God who gave you power over sin. He did not perform these miraculous events because these Bible characters were perfect; he did it because they put their trust in him.

Moses and David were both murderers (read Ex 2: 11-15 and 2 Sam: 11). By law, God should have struck them down for killing another person. Instead, he was a friend and showed loving kindness to them. Earlier in scripture, God showed the same mercy to Abraham, Isaac, and Jacob when they went down the wrong path. God is no respecter of persons. If you have a repentant heart, he will forgive you no matter how many mistakes you've made.

God stays true to his word and it never returns void. He watches over his word and will continue doing so in the future until he returns for his people (John 14:3). Jesus came (past tense) to this earth more than two thousand years ago to save us from eternal damnation due to sin, to give (present tense) us an abundant life, and he will (future tense) come back to gather his saints to be with him in glory. We can rest in knowing Jesus will never change.

FASTEN YOUR FAITH

- Thank God that he is consistent in your life.
- Believe God loves you, including when you mess up.
- Pray for a great miracle in your life.

You are Holy

Therefore, be imitators of God as dear children.
-Ephesians 5:1, NKJV

If I let my guard down by doing whatever I want to do, my old self tends to creep back in. I find myself watching garbage, listening to trash and saying distasteful words. The immediate gratification satisfies me but I cannot shake off the feeling of being dirty and uncomfortable on the inside. I feel like the inner stains I produced are penetrating through my soul and onto my clothes for everyone to see.

As filthy as I may feel, I know it is a good thing. I am grieving the Holy Spirit and he in turn is convicting me of my sins. In hindsight, my behavior may not appear to be wrong. But if the Lord tells me to refrain from something and I do it anyway it is sin. If the Lord tells me to do something and I refuse, it is sin as well. Even delayed obedience is still disobedience.

Grieving the Holy Spirit is the worst part of all. Who would willingly stomp on goodness, kindness and mercy? But that is exactly what we are doing when we intentionally sin. Christians are a peculiar people, a royal priesthood and God wants us to live according to his ways. We are bought with a price and sealed unto the day of redemption and we are to act like it by being imitators of Christ.

So, get excited for the icky feeling that you get when you are not living right because it is God calling you to a higher standard of living. He wants to wash you through the water of his word so you can live with a clean conscience, a clean heart and clean hands. God loves us too much to allow us to continue to live in our mess.

FASTEN YOUR FAITH

- Confess if there is a particular sin that you have become accustomed to.
- Ask the Holy Spirit to give you the icky feeling whenever you sin to help you walk in obedience to him.
- Refuse to settle for a lower standard of living.

God Listens to You

All those who truly respected the Lord and honored
his name started discussing these things, and
when God saw what was happening, he had their
names written as a reminder in his book.
-Malachi 3:16, CEV

God is listening to everything we say. For those with an untamed tongue, it can be convicting to know that God is listening to every conversation. All the gossip, cursing and lying we may do is heard, and one day, that conduct will be confronted by Jesus himself at the Judgement Seat of Christ. On the other hand, every time we talk about God in a positive light, or share a testimony of his goodness, he gets excited and writes down our names in a book of remembrance.

Sometimes, I am afraid to talk to other people about God for whatever reason. Most of the time, I am mainly afraid that I will be brushed off or that my "reputation" will be ruined. But knowing that God pays attention to what I say about him excites me. I am motivated to be more vocal about him in a natural and genuine way. God is listening, and that is all that matters.

FASTEN YOUR FAITH

- Talk to at least one person about God today.
- Ask God to help you discipline your tongue.
- Look up scriptures about the Judgement Seat of Christ.

God Comes Through for You

I would have lost heart, unless I had believed that I would
see the goodness of the Lord in the land of the living.
-Psalms 27:13, NKJV

Like King David, you may be going through a trying time in your life. It may seem as if life itself is against you. Nothing is going right. Every time you take a step forward, you experience a setback that takes you three steps backwards. David knew he would be king one day but at this point in his life, he was living in the wilderness and fleeing for his life from King Saul. Saul was jealous of David's popularity and favor. David was tempted to lose all hope, but he put his trust in the Lord. He knew this season in his life would pass.

It took David more than ten years to get out of his wilderness experience. Some scholars believe it was approximately fifteen years, but this journey allowed David to develop the character and resilience he needed to be a good king. He is hands down, one of the most popular kings to this day.

During David's most trying times, he encouraged himself with declarations, poems and songs that he made and dedicated to the Lord. He wrote his most popular pieces during this timeframe. The famous Psalms 23 and Palms 121 poems were produced during this wilderness experience in his life.

David did not give up and neither should we, no matter how hard life may try to knock us down. God is the author of our lives. He is writing the story. After we make it through, we will look back and see how everything (the good, the bad and the ugly) propelled us into our destiny.

FASTEN YOUR FAITH

- If your dream hasn't come to pass yet, ask God to help you trust the process.
- Speak life over yourself instead of speaking negativity.
- Ask God to give you a great comeback for every setback you are facing.

 *18*

God Reveals His Will

In everything give thanks, for this is the
will of God in Christ Jesus for you.
-1 Thessalonians 5:18, NKJV

My best friend knew that she was supposed to become a doctor since the tender age of four years old. She knew that's what God specifically wanted her to do with her life for his glory. As she got older, people tried to persuade her to take easier routes, like becoming a physician assistant or nurse practitioner (easier pertaining to the number of years needed for school). As tempting as it was to go veer off-track, she never swayed from what God wanted her to do. She is now a pediatrician, in her last year of residency, and walking in her purpose.

For me, trying to figure out my purpose, or God's specific will for my life, doesn't come that easy. I have to pray, seek and fast. You see, I did not grow up seeking the Lord's will and now life has already happened to me. I have bills, debts and doubts that constantly drown out whatever hopes and dreams God placed in my heart for me to carry out.

When I get in my feelings of doubt that God won't reveal his will to me, I'm reminded that I do know his will for my life (or at least part of it). He always guides me back to the scripture, 1 Thess: 5:18. It says, "In everything, give thanks, for this is the will of God in Christ Jesus for you." I know my purpose is to give thanks to God in everything I do and experience. I am grateful the Lord is ordering my steps and vows to take me wherever I am supposed to go.

FASTEN YOUR FAITH

- Do what you already know to do (i.e., read your Bible, pray, go to church, be kind to others).
- Ask God to reveal his purpose for your life despite the fact that life already happened to you.
- Rely on the power of the Holy Spirit to begin or to continue carrying out God's will.

God's Favor Sustains You

For his anger endureth but a moment; in
his favor is life: weeping may endure for a
night, but joy comes in the morning.
-Ps 30:5, KJV

I tossed and turned in bed one night because I started thinking about how I have more bills than money. I did not want to wallow in my feelings for too long, so I decided to look up scriptures about joy on the Bible app I had downloaded. The first scripture about joy that I came to was Ps: 30:5. It reads, "For his anger is but for a moment; in his favor is life. Weeping may endure for a night, but joy comes in the morning.

This time, when I read the verse, the words *in his favor is life* popped out at me. *Favor* and *life* are such powerful words. According to Webster, favor means overgenerous preferential treatment, and life means vitality, vigor and energy. Man, that's good! God's favor gives us everything we need to live life as he intended.

You can walk confidently through life knowing his overgenerous preferential treatment is coming your way.

FASTEN YOUR FAITH

- Look for God's favor in your life today.
- Remind yourself that life is worth living.
- Download a Bible app onto your phone or tablet and use it to look up scriptures throughout your day.

All You Need is in Christ

*And my God shall supply all your need according
to His riches in glory by Christ Jesus.
-Philippians 4:19, NKJV*

If you are a working mom like me, you can understand when I say that six weeks of maternity leave is not enough time to fully transition from pregnancy, to life with your new baby. But a short maternity leave is the norm in our work-driven society.

When I returned to work after my first baby, I felt guilty that I was going back to work so soon, but financially, I did not have the option to stay home. I cried leaving the house because I felt as if I was choosing work over my child. I did not want to do that the second time around, so I decided to take advantage of the Family Medical Leave Act, which legally allowed me to get twelve weeks off. The only problem is FMLA only protects you from losing your job during your time off. Whatever is not covered by your employer during that time is unpaid. Although my husband and I did not have enough money for the remaining time I would have off, I knew taking the extra time was what I needed to do.

So, I took the twelve weeks off and started my maternity leave. As I moved into the unpaid weeks of my maternity leave, one of my husband's former clients randomly sent us a one thousand dollar check in the mail. They were unaware of our financial situation but the check they sent covered all of the remaining bills we needed to pay.

My jaw dropped when we opened the envelope. I wanted to scream from the rooftop and tell everyone about our little but big miracle that I just witnessed. I could not believe it, and at the same time, I could believe it! The Lord supplied all our needs according to his riches in glory by Christ Jesus.

FASTEN YOUR FAITH

- Present all your needs to Jesus.
- Decide to trust Jesus based on what he said and not what you see or feel.
- Pray for clarity and understanding when making financial decisions.

Questions for Reflection

1. What is your favorite meditation so far and why?

2. Have you applied any of these meditations (11-20) to your week? Was there any difference in how you approached your day as a result?

3. Has the Lord changed your outlook on what it means to walk by faith and not by sight? Explain.

4. How have you experienced the Lord's favor this week?

5. Have you shared your testimony with someone?

Reflection Notes

God Cares About the Little Things

…Casting all your care upon Him, for He cares for you.
-1 Pet 5:7, NKJV

Asking God to help you find your phone or misplaced keys may not be the first thing that comes to your mind when it comes to casting your cares on him. It is easy to think God has more important things to worry about, like healing someone from an incurable disease, or comforting someone during a time of loss.

I often reminisce on my visit to see my boyfriend, now husband, for the weekend when he lived in Toledo, Ohio, and I resided in Cleveland, Ohio. He really wanted me to see his baseball game before I left, but there was a ninety-nine percent chance of rain on the day of his game. I told him to pray that it would not rain and he laughed. He pretty much said that God does not care about little stuff like that. So, I said a prayer under my breath asking the Lord to stop it from raining the next day to show my husband that He does care about every detail of his life.

Low and behold, there was no rain whatsoever the next day, and I got to see his baseball game. As I was leaving to go back home, I looked directly into my husband's eyes and told him to never forget that day. I said, "It was supposed to rain but the Lord stopped the rain just to prove that he does care about the little things in your life." You can truly bring everything to the Lord in prayer.

Fasten Your Faith

- Bring your cares to Jesus as soon as they occur and not as a last resort.
- Casting means rolling or throwing onto something. Avoid picking up your care after you've already thrown it onto the Lord.
- Remember that God cares about every detail in your life.

You are Already Free

Therefore if the Son makes you free, you shall be free indeed.
-John 8:36, NKJV

Pornography is an addiction that a lot of people struggle with. Although it is more prevalent with men, a lot of women struggle with it too. It can come in the form of videos, books, toys—the whole nine yards. Those addicted to porn are rewarded with a false reality in addition to instant gratification. But when that video or chapter is over with, they have to snap back to reality. As their appetite is continually satisfied, the ability to shift back from the false reality gets harder and harder.

This is something I struggled with as well. I was introduced to pornography in high school, and it continued when I went to college. I rededicated my life to Christ in college, but I still struggled with this issue. I could not stop even though I prayed for the desire to go away. One day I got fed up and declared I was not falling prey to porn anymore because Jesus had already set me free. I haven't looked back since.

My disgust for pornography overpowered my lust for pornography once I identified my actions as sin and not simply as an addiction or human nature. I was able to boldly proclaim God's word and allow the Lord to give me the victory in this area of my life. God said he always gives us a way to escape our temptations. He also said we are no longer slaves to the power of sin because of what he did on the cross. He already set you free. The question is, do you want to be?

FASTEN YOUR FAITH

- Ask yourself if you truly want to be free from whatever stronghold you may have.
- Boldly declare God's word over your situation.
- Take the escape route when you encounter temptation.

Showing Hospitality Blesses You

*Do not forget to entertain strangers, for by so doing
some have unwittingly entertained angels.*
-Hebrews 13:2, NKJV

Lot was a man of God even though he lived in the sin city
of his time: Sodom. He adamantly looked for ways to
bless others. When Lot saw two foreigners enter at the
city gate, he greeted them and invited them to his house
to eat and to stay overnight to rest. Even when they
initially said no, he convinced them that he genuinely
wanted to show them some southern hospitality.

By reading the story in Genesis 19, we know Lot
was entertaining angels but in his eyes he was entertaining
strangers. He had no idea whom he was serving. During
dinner, the angels warned him the town was about to
come under God's judgment and he needed to leave
immediately. It was a lot for Lot to digest, and he hesitated
from leaving. The angels literally dragged Lot and his

family out of the area before the Lord rained down his judgment.

No one coerced Lot to go out of his way to be nice. He could have simply waved and kept moving. Lot intentionally blessed these "strangers," and he ended up being blessed by them. Lot's hospitality saved his life.

FASTEN YOUR FAITH

- Pray for a hospitable heart.
- Show unusual kindness to someone today.
- Go the extra mile with others.

Your Superpower is Joy

"...Do not sorrow, for the joy of the Lord is your strength."
-Nehemiah 8:10, NKJV

When interviewing for a position, a common thing the interviewer says is, "Tell me about your strengths and weaknesses." Any serious candidate knows this is going to come up at some point in the interview, and they will dedicate a good amount of time thinking about what they will say. Polished candidates may even tie in their weakness as an actual strength.

For believers, one of our greatest strengths is having the joy of the Lord. Joy is a fruit of the Spirit that is cultivated from personally knowing Jesus and having his mindset. Joy is different from being happy because happiness is dictated on the external—things that are happening around you. When things are going good around you, you in turn feel good on the inside. The catch is, it's all based on feelings. The happiness you experience will fade away whenever your feelings change; good or bad.

Joy, on the other hand, is dictated on the internal—something from within you that manifests externally. When good things come your way, you have an inner peace and anticipation. When bad things come your way, you still keep the same disposition. Letdowns in life could be health-related, job-related or people-related. Just know it does not have to change you. With joy, you can always look on the bright side. With joy your cup is always half-full instead of half-empty. Keep your eyes on Jesus and you will always find a reason to smile.

FASTEN YOUR FAITH

- Claim the joy of the Lord over your life today.
- Spend time talking with Jesus throughout your day.
- Pray for a heavenly mindset.

God Enhances Your Life

For the Lord God is a sun and shield; the Lord
will give grace and mercy; No good thing will He
withhold from them who walk uprightly.
-Psalms 84:11, NKJV

Some people believe living for God will cause them to lose out on experiencing or obtaining certain things they want in life. They think God does not want them to have their dream job, ideal spouse, luxury vehicle, etc. It can be pretty scary putting your hopes and dreams into the hands of someone else. What if you want to be married but Jesus wants you to remain single? What if you want to retire and relocate to a nice area but Jesus wants you to keep working or become a missionary? Anything can fall into the "what if" category, but it is fear that God will prevent us from having something good in our lives.

When I read this verse, I think about the story of the Hebrew midwives, Shiphrah and Puah, who lived in Egypt during the era of Moses. Pharaoh ordered these ladies to kill all the baby boys they helped deliver, but they feared God and did not listen to Pharaoh's orders. Pharaoh was angry but God was pleased. The Bible says God was good to them and he provided households for them, which is a family of their own. (Ex 1:21).

The Bible does not say the women specifically asked for a husband and kids but God knew it was good for their lives. God already knew the desires of their hearts by their actions. Shiphrah and Puah valued family and children because they risked their own lives to save other people's children. They also stayed true to their beliefs and values at the risk of losing their careers. These women walked uprightly before the Lord, and he honored their courageous stance by giving them something that specifically enhanced their lives.

FASTEN YOUR FAITH

- Believe God will withhold no good thing from you.
- Stay true to your non-negotiables.
- Pray for courage to walk uprightly.

God Loves You Despite Your Failures

...for they all shall know Me, from the least of them to the greatest of them, says the Lord.
-Jeremiah 31:34, NKJV

I participated in a lot of activities throughout high school. I joined the flag line and dance line in the marching band, played the violin in the orchestra, and I played on the volleyball and softball team. Although I am very competitive, I was never the all-star of the team. Greatness did not come naturally for me in those areas, like it seemed to for others. One girl in my graduating class was great at everything she did. She participated in nearly every school activity you could think of and she excelled in them all. She was so good that she received athletic scholarship offers in almost every sport. However, I was just happy to make the team.

As long as you are alive, there will always be someone better, smarter and more attractive than you. This is a fact of life. That is why the Lord made the distinction in saying from the least of them unto the greatest. Whether you come in first place, fifth place or last place, your accomplishments or lack thereof will not change God's love towards you.

As long you serve with all your heart, mind and soul, that is enough for God. He will not treat you any differently if you are not the best. Instead of focusing on being the best at something, focus on being the best version of yourself and having the best relationship with Jesus that you can.

FASTEN YOUR FAITH

- Strive to be the best version of yourself.
- Put your worth in God and not in your accomplishments.
- Avoid comparing yourself to others.

God Defends You

*Beloved, do not avenge yourselves, but rather
give place to wrath; for it is written, "Vengeance
is Mine, I will repay," says the Lord.*
-Romans 12:19, NKJV

Before David was king, he found himself and his crew
in the wilderness fleeing for their lives from King Saul.
During this time, David and his men came across a group
of men tending sheep. Being a shepherd boy at heart,
David protected the animals and workers from any danger
that came their way. David knew all those sheep belonged
to someone wealthy, and after investigating, he discovered
they belonged to a man named Nabal. When sheep-
shearing season arrived, David sent some of his men to
Nabal's home to see if he would spare some food as a favor
for the kindness David showed.

In David's mind, he knew Nabal would say yes and
ultimately become one of his allies. Instead, Nabal sneered
at David and his men and turned them away empty-
handed. David was outraged and set out to destroy Nabal,

along with anyone associated with him. He did not care that innocent people would die in the process. He was ready for war.

David was en route when Nabal's wife, Abigail, found out what transpired. She immediately journeyed to meet up with David. She provided food and took the blame for her husband's actions. Abigail also reminded David of a truth: "Vengeance is mine," says the Lord. David quickly came to his senses and retreated from his plan of killing Nabal.

A few days later, David heard Nabal had died from a heart attack. God struck Nabal and vindicated David indeed. David in turn rejoiced because he did not take matters into his own hands. He even took Abigail as his wife.

FASTEN YOUR FAITH

- Ask the Lord to bring you to your senses when you are ready to take matters into your own hands.
- Listen to the Abigails in your life.
- Keep a good attitude if your hopes are deferred.

God Sets the Stage

And we know that all things work together
for good to those who love God, to those who
are the called according to His purpose.
-Romans 8:28, NKJV

Job was a man that had it all. He was very wealthy, had a great family, people respected him and most of all, he was a man who loved and honored God. But in one day, nearly everything he had was snatched away. His animals were stolen, his workers were killed and all of his children died in a fire. Job's health even declined and boils covered his entire body. It got so bad that his wife said, "Curse God and die." Job responded by saying, "Though he slay me, yet will I trust him" (Job 13:15).

God already knew what was going on; in fact, he recommended Job to Satan. God gave Satan permission to do whatever he wanted to do in Job's life. The devil wanted to prove to God that people (in this case Job) only loved God for the blessings he provides. Satan's argument was, if people had everything taken away from them, they would blame God and stop loving and serving him.

God knew Job would stay true to him. He used Job's life to prove Satan wrong. When the temptation subsided, God restored everything Job lost. Job experienced more blessings in every area of his life than he ever did before the traumatic events took place. The Bible says he died old and full of days. He enjoyed his life to the fullest.

FASTEN YOUR FAITH

- Ask God to give you a true love for him and not just the blessings you can get from him.
- Know that the devil needs permission from God to do anything in your life.
- Thank God for recommending you and recognize that he equipped you to pass the tests and trials in your life.

Your Spirit Never Dies

Therefore we do not lose heart. Even though
our outward man is perishing, yet the inward
man is being renewed day by day.
-2 Corinthians 4:16, NAS

I wish I could stay young forever but growing old and eventually dying is inevitable. Originally, the human race was not created to wither away and perish, but now we are required to die as a result of Adam's fall in the Garden of Eden and the introduction of sin (disobedience to God).

In our youth, we may take the pep in our step for granted. We can pull all-nighters, binge watch our favorite television shows, or stuff our faces with unhealthy food and still manage to stay slim. As we age, it's another story. Our health, outward appearance and physical strength will not be at one hundred percent as it previously was.

Although death is inescapable, we can stay young in our inner man because our spirit never dies. King David talked about aging in Psalms 71. He asked the Lord to remember him as he approached his golden years. David prayed for comprehension and against confusion. He wanted to continually praise the Lord, just like he did in his youth. We too can ask God for the same things David did so we can age with dignity and grace.

Fasten Your Faith

- Discuss growing old with the Lord.
- Take proper steps to prepare for your death (i.e., life insurance, will, retirement, etc.).
- Ask God to renew your inner man no matter how old you are.

You're a Living Vessel

Flee also youthful lusts; but pursue righteousness, faith, love, peace, with those who call on the Lord out of a pure heart.
-2 Timothy 2: 22, NKJV

The book of Timothy is a letter Paul wrote specifically to Timothy. Timothy was a very young believer entrusted with the preaching and teaching of God's word. Paul took him under his wing and mentored him into a strong leader. He encouraged Timothy in various ways, especially by admonishing him to not let anyone despise him due to his age. Before finishing, Paul also presented Timothy with landmines to watch out for.

Youthful lusts were one of the main landmines. Youthful lusts are things that can latch onto your soul and has the ability to grip the heart of your emotions, thoughts and actions. Fulfilling selfish indulgences, desiring someone else's life, and self-centered ambitions all fall into the youthful lust category.

If you take the path of youthful lusts, it leads to becoming a vessel of dishonor, as described in 2

Timothy Chapter 2. Satan uses the cares of this world as a distraction to lure believers away from the direction of the Holy Spirit, eventually making the servant of God useless. Satisfaction with your own plans and accomplishments verses God's plans is quintessentially fool's gold.

Paul showed Timothy how to tiptoe around youthful lusts by encouraging him to follow after righteousness, faith, love and peace. These steps are prerequisites to becoming a vessel of honor. Vessels of honor may not necessarily look honorable. Eleven out of Jesus's twelve disciples, Martin Luther King, Jr. and even Paul were martyred for being obedient vessels. They gave up living long enjoyable lives in exchange for dying a horrible death.

Their deaths allowed God's will to be done at that point in history. When you live as a vessel of honor, the glory of the Lord is always at bay.

FASTEN YOUR FAITH

- Do you consider yourself a vessel of honor or dishonor at this point in your life? Decrease so he may increase.
- Confess and surrender any youthful lusts you may have to God.
- Ask the Lord to mold you into a faithful servant, even to the point of death.

Questions for Reflection

1. What is your overall favorite meditation? Why?

2. Have you applied any of these meditations (20-30) to your week? Was there any difference in how you approached your day as a result?

3. How are you becoming the best version of yourself?

4. Are you communing with God on a regular basis?

5. Are you afraid of dying? Why or why not?

Reflection Notes

Epilogue

As important as it is to fasten your faith belt, it is more important to know what vehicle you're in and where you are headed. In this book, I use my testimonies and other inspirational stories to strengthen the faith of a believer. If you are not saved (have not personally asked for Jesus's salvation or given your life to Christ by recognizing you are a sinner and in need of a savior) then your faith is altogether on the wrong track because there is no harness in the "slave to sin" automobile you are riding in. The "slave to sin" car is set on autopilot down the road that leads to eternal separation from God, which is hell.

Jesus describes hell in detail by using the story of the rich man and Lazarus in Luke 16:19-31. The rich man lived a carefree life on earth, and when he died, he immediately went to hell, while Lazarus died and instantly went to heaven. The Bible says the rich man cried out saying, "Have mercy on me and send Lazarus that he may dip the tip of his finger in cool water, for I am tormented in this flame.

Hell is a real place and that is where we all deserve to go if we break just one of God's commandments. God loves us and doesn't want anyone to perish, so he provided a map for everyone to follow that leads to salvation. This map is called the Romans Road. Please proceed to read the following scriptures:

- <u>Romans 3:23</u>: For we all have sinned and come short of the glory of God.

- <u>Romans 6: 23</u>: For the wages of sin is death, but the gift of God is eternal life through Jesus Christ our Lord.

- <u>Romans 5:8</u>: But God demonstrates his own love for us in this: While we were still sinners, Christ died for us.

- <u>Romans 10:9</u>: That if you confess with your mouth, "Jesus is Lord," and believe in your heart that God raised him from the dead, you will be saved. For it is with your heart that you believe and are justified, and it is with your mouth that you confess and are saved.

- <u>Romans 10:13</u>: For "whoever calls on the name of the Lord shall be saved."

- <u>Romans 8:1</u>: Therefore, there is now no condemnation for those who are in Christ Jesus, because through Christ Jesus the law of the Spirit of life set me free from the law of sin and death.

If you recited those scriptures and want to give your life to Christ, pray this prayer with me:

Dear Jesus. I come to you, acknowledging that I am a sinner and I'm in need of a savior. You are the only one who can save me from my sins because you, who are without sin, willingly paid the price for me. I believe you died on the cross and you rose again with all power in your hands. Today, I turn from my life of sin and pledge my allegiance to you. As of now, I'm no longer a sinner but a saint who is covered by your precious blood. Thank you for saving me, in Jesus's name, amen.

If you believe in your heart what you just prayed, then you are now saved. Hallelujah! Tell someone about your commitment to Christ and take the steps to join a Bible-teaching church.

Now that you are headed in the right direction, remember to intentionally fasten your faith belt every day of your Christian walk. Girding yourself up protects you from the enemy and from yourself. No matter what comes your way, your trust in Jesus will never waver. You will be steadfast, unmovable, always abounding in the work of the Lord.

May God bless you and keep you and shine his face upon you all the days of your life.

Acknowledgments

First, I would like to start by thanking my Lord and Savior, Jesus Christ. Thanks for putting the desire within me to create this book for your people. Even when I stopped dreaming of becoming an author, you never let my childhood dream die. I love you and no one compares to you.

Next, I would like to thank my husband and closest friend, Joshua Emanuel Smith. You motivate me to turn my dreams into a reality. You are truly a gift from God.

To my children, Saniyah and Braylon, I want to be everything God called me to be, so I can lead by example and pave the way for you two to do the same.

To my parents, Maurice and Rennota Smith, and to my mother-in-love, Diane Smith, thank you for being the best parents a girl could ever have.

I would like to thank my brother, Tyler Smith, for always being there for me.

I would also like to thank all my family, friends and church family who had a positive influence in my walk with God.

I would like to give a special thanks to Tarshree' Sawyer and B'Nai Townes, who are my best friends and accountability partners.

And last but not least, to my friend Erica Arnold, thank you for encouraging me through every step of this process.

More from the Author

Breana Smith serves in full-time ministry at New Community Bible Fellowship, a non-denominational church, located in Cleveland Heights, Ohio. There, she manages the reception office and supports the Administration, Christian Education, and Membership Care departments.

Breana obtained a Bachelor's Degree in Journalism from Bowling Green State University. During her time at BGSU, Breana served on the leadership team of Impact Ministries, a student-led campus Bible study under the umbrella of CRU (Campus Crusades for Christ). Within that organization, she taught young adult men and women how to love God by applying his word to their daily lives.

Breana was also heavily involved with L.I.F.E. Ministries, which means Living in Faith Every day. This campus Bible study operated under the teaching of Jerry Hunt, pastor of Word of Truth Christian Center in Bowling Green, Ohio.

For additional resources or to book Breana for your next event, visit her online at www.breanajsmith.com.

16707136R00046

Made in the USA
Middletown, DE
02 December 2018